Mama Bear Says
POCKET WISDOM

HEATHER DAKOTA

ISBN: 978-1-955346-02-3

10 9 8 7 6 5 4 3 2 1

Layout & Cover Design by Heather Dakota
Illustrations by Heather Dakota

Published by Wyrd & Wyld Publishing; Spokane, WA

www.heatherdakota.com

To all Beings
seeking comfort, answers, belonging,
or a direction. You are seen. You are heard.
You are held in the arms of Mama Bear.

Mama Bear Says

POCKET WISDOM

BY

HEATHER DAKOTA

MAMA BEAR SAYS HELLO

Greetings Beautiful Soul,

As Mama Bear sits in her cave, she opens her arms wide for all the Beings who need her healing and nurturing magic.

Mama Bear stands us up, dusts us off, and gives us a knowing in our bones to expect the beauty of life to unfold.

Ultimate freedom beckons as Mama Bear's wisdom fuels the mind with positive thoughts and experiences for this one amazing life. The world may feel harsh, divided, and without empathy or compassion, but we are all in this together.

Mama Bear has a big lap and wide arms to hold us all. Step up and ask for her support, and she'll be there with her loving embrace ready to hear about your pain and sorrow, happiness and joy.

This beautiful Being is motivated by love and infused with a nurturing energy that comes from understanding the profound laws of connection.

Bears are the healers of the spiritual realm—gentle and loving and fierce protectors when needed. Mama Bear lumbers through our realm, claims adequate rest, nurtures, and shares her wisdom. She embodies a motherly grace, and her magic allows a safe space for self-reflection.

Mama Bear's dream is that these words are a light in dark places for those who carry them and her wisdom integrates into the collective for better understanding and compassion for one another. When doubts creep in that undermine our trust and confidence, Mama Bear's wisdom flows with love and kindness.

The content of *Mama Bear Says* is not a substitute for therapy. Mama Bear and I are not experts in psychology or behavior, but we both believe that we can learn from nature and the gifts of spirit.

This book is offered as a golden compass when you're in murky territory and self-compassion is required.

Mama Bear and I hope you enjoy cultivating your own Mama Bear wisdom. May you always be held in her loving and nurturing energy.

Many Blessings and Radiant Magic,
Heather & Mama Bear

How to Use This Book

We give so much to others that we often forget about ourselves. Mama Bear invites you into discovery with prompts for strength and fortitude to take care of yourself, meet your needs, and nurture your creativity, health, happiness, and joy.

There are several ways to work with this book.

Read it cover-to-cover

Start at the beginning and read the book all the way through. Mama Bear's energy is nurturing and nourishing. Work with her energy to soothe your worries and fears and bring the high-energy of everyday life back into alignment with the natural world and who you truly are.

As a Meditation or Journal Practice

Sit quietly with Mama Bear and allow her energy to infuse your body, mind, heart, and soul. Like a soothing balm, Mama Bear's mighty arms are here to hold and protect you. Choose one of the pages to sit with during your spiritual practice. Mama Bear has the answers you seek. She is in touch with your higher self and intuition, and the ancient wisdom of the ages. When you need guidance, call on her in meditation.

As a Creative Practice

Take a prompt into your creative practice. Create mixed media, artwork, or story. Use colored pencils to color these pages. Use your intuition to make marks, add color or images. Anything you create is perfect. If you feel called, share with others on social media **#mamabearsays** Let your light shine!

As An Oracle

Mama Bear is filled with the magic and wisdom of the ancient ones. When you are seeking an answer or knowledge for a decision, Mama Bear divines for you. Flip to a random page for the answer you seek.

MAMA BEAR
INVOCATION

I call to the womb cave of creation
to sense, feel, and awaken
the soothing nurture of Mama Bear
in my body, mind, heart, and soul.
I call on Mama Bear's strength
to help me walk in serenity,
so I may emerge from her embrace
with warmth, love, and caring
for others and myself.
May every moment I breathe
embody Mama Bear's wisdom.
May my pain and fear
be comforted in her loving arms.
May each step I take
be a prayer of connection to *All That Is*.
May my own Mama Bear intuition
move me to act with integrity and grace.
May I celebrate, inspire, and empower others
through the love and warmth
Mama Bear has shown me.

Mama Bear Says

Celebrate who you are today.

MAMA BEAR SAYS

Listen to your heartbeat.

MAMA BEAR SAYS

Take a day to be alone
with who you really are.

Mama Bear Says

You are seen.
You are heard.
You are loved.
Mama Bear's energy
holds you and keeps you.

MAMA BEAR SAYS

Talk to your soul.
What does it need right now?

Mama Bear Says

Have a good cry to
cleanse your soul.

MAMA BEAR SAYS

Let go of being perfect.
It isn't attainable.

MAMA BEAR SAYS

Let go of the past.

Mama Bear Says

Do not worry about the future.
It hasn't happened yet.
You only have this moment.

MAMA BEAR SAYS

Seek solitude.

Mama Bear Says

Tell the truth, gently.

MAMA BEAR SAYS

The energy of Mother Earth
is within you.
Step into this power.

Mama Bear Says

Your body is beautiful.

MAMA BEAR SAYS

Be your ideal partner.

MAMA BEAR SAYS

Take a social media sabbatical.

Mama Bear Says

Go all day
without giving excuses.

Mama Bear Says

The river shows us
how to flow within
the confines and
structure of the banks.

MAMA BEAR SAYS

Admit when you're wrong.

MAMA BEAR SAYS

Let go of expectations.

Mama Bear Says

You have permission
to want what you want.

Mama Bear Says

Listen to your intuition.
It is your inner compass
for what comes next.

MAMA BEAR SAYS

Be gentle with yourself,
as if you were
a child of the Universe,
because you are.

Mama Bear Says

Give yourself another chance.

Mama Bear Says

You did not fail.
You gained experience.

MAMA BEAR SAYS

Sleep in.

MAMA BEAR SAYS

Eat by candlelight,
even if you're alone.

MAMA BEAR SAYS

You have my permission
to say *NO*.

MAMA BEAR SAYS

Be in your body.
Name 5 things you see.
Name 4 things you hear.
Name 3 things you smell.
Name 2 things you feel.
Name 1 thing you taste.

MAMA BEAR SAYS

Take up space.

Mama Bear Says

Trust yourself, even if
you've let yourself down before.

Mama Bear Says

Be bored. This is where
possibilities reside.

Mama Bear Says

Come child. Take time to play today.

Mama Bear Says

Trust your inner wisdom.

Mama Bear Says

Throw out the to-do list and follow your own energy to the land of enchantment.

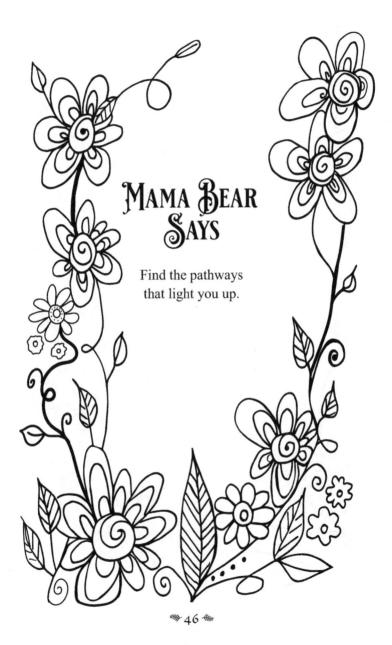

MAMA BEAR SAYS

Find the pathways
that light you up.

MAMA BEAR SAYS

Take a nap.
Rest your body today.

MAMA BEAR SAYS

Drink a cup of warm tea
to soothe your soul and warm your bones.

Mama Bear Says

Let go of control
just this once and drink in the
wild unknown.

Mama Bear Says

Be happy with
your enoughness.

Mama Bear Says

What will make your body feel
nourished, healthy, and strong?
If you don't know,
explore and discover.

MAMA BEAR SAYS

Romance yourself. Buy yourself flowers.

Mama Bear Says

You work so hard. It's time
to get off the hamster wheel,
if only for today.

MAMA BEAR SAYS

What do you want
your morning routine to look like?
A simple routine has a big impact.

Mama Bear Says

What evening routine
do you want to implement?
Invite your dreams.

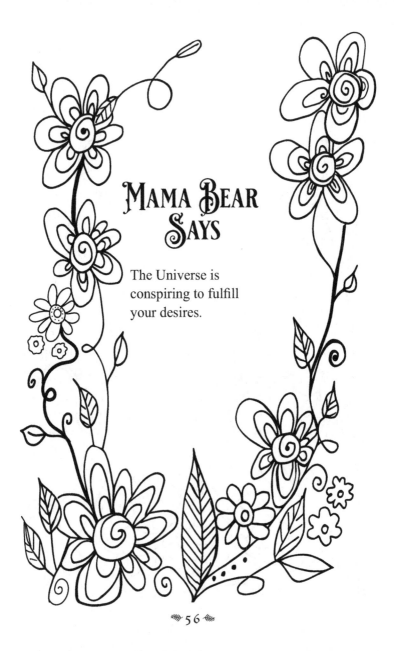

MAMA BEAR SAYS

The Universe is conspiring to fulfill your desires.

Mama Bear Says

Honor all Beings today,
even the ones you don't agree
with. I know it's difficult.
Come to me when you need
comfort from the fray.

Mama Bear Says

How much space does your
mind, body, heart, or soul
need today?
What must be released?

Mama Bear Says

Take the time to clear and release the physical, emotional, mental, and spiritual cobwebs for a fresh start.

Mama Bear Says

Put your faith, power, and
trust in the natural world.

Mama Bear Says

Build strong foundations locally.

MAMA BEAR SAYS

Get to know your neighbors.
Build community.

Mama Bear Says

Feel the soil beneath your
feet as a solid foundation.

Mama Bear Says

There are stars in your eyes
that hold the vision of the
celestial realms and all Beings.
What will you do with what
you see?

Mama Bear Says

Create a cozy and serene place to escape the stress of a chaotic world. Go there as often as you need.

MAMA BEAR SAYS

Stay in your pajamas all day.

Mama Bear Says

Go without electronics today.
Turn off your phone.
Turn off the TV.
Turn off the lights.
Bathe yourself in
candlelight and stillness.

Mama Bear Says

Stretch and move your body.
Release your stagnant energy
with powerful poses, dancing,
and silly movements.

Mama Bear Says

Make an offering of your tears.
Mother Earth holds
them sacred.

Mama Bear Says

The Universe
is always guiding you.
Listen to the wind.
Listen to the birds.
Listen to the trees.
Listen. Listen. Listen.

MAMA BEAR SAYS

Smile at everyone you meet.
We're all doing
the best we can.

Mama Bear Says

Be happy with enough.

MAMA BEAR SAYS

Nurture yourself today.
You are not selfish.
You are being kind to you.

MAMA BEAR SAYS

Celebrate the cycles and
rhythms of this blessed life.

MAMA BEAR SAYS

Slow down
to the speed of nature.
Notice every-little-thing.

MAMA BEAR SAYS

Look for what the ancestors planted
in your DNA that is ready to be
introduced to the world.

MAMA BEAR SAYS

If you're happy and you
know it, clap you hands.

MAMA BEAR SAYS

Take time for introspection.

MAMA BEAR SAYS

Don't compare yourself to others.
Trust your own heart.

MAMA BEAR SAYS

Mama Bear loves you
no matter what.

MAMA BEAR SAYS

It's okay to change your mind.

Mama Bear Says

When a door closes,
look for the open window.
See all opportunities with
sacred eyes.

MAMA BEAR SAYS

Look at the stars tonight.
Because of all the places
in all the Universe,
you are miracle right here.

MAMA BEAR SAYS

You are needed and wanted.

Mama Bear Says

Don't quit before the miracle.

MAMA BEAR SAYS

Seed of wonder.
Star of light.
Fear and worry
be gone tonight.

Mama Bear Says

Enter the healing cave.

Mama Bear Says

Live in the present moment,
instead of in the stories of the past
or worries of the future.

Mama Bear Says

Celebrate who you are
and your connection to the cosmos.
Bless the lineage from which you came.

Mama Bear Says

You are in control
of this one beautiful life.

MAMA BEAR SAYS

Believe in magic!
You are the magic.

MAMA BEAR SAYS

Today is a good day to be alive.
So was Yesterday and
Tomorrow will be, too.

MAMA BEAR SAYS

It's okay to sit in
the in between.
When you're ready,
the wisdom or knowledge
will show up.

MAMA BEAR SAYS

The Universe is conspiring
on your behalf.
You are worthy.
Trust in Divine timing.

MAMA BEAR SAYS

Your words are powerful!
Write down what you want
or desire in a positive way.
I want… I desire…

Mama Bear Says

Let go of expectations.
Sometimes they are rules
disguised as goals.

Mama Bear Says

Celebrate your efforts
as well as your accomplishments.

MAMA BEAR SAYS

Explore your life for the
golden threads to weave a
blanket of joy.

Mama Bear Says

Do not dwell in the past.
You've already lived there.
Do not worry about the future.
It hasn't happened yet.
Be happy in this moment,
for it is all you truly have.

MAMA BEAR SAYS

With experience comes
wisdom and knowledge.

MAMA BEAR SAYS

Cherish the profound wisdom
you have within you.

MAMA BEAR SAYS

Today is for daydreaming.

MAMA BEAR SAYS

Do something today that thrills you.

Mama Bear Says

You are only a character in
other people's stories,
not responsible for the plot.

MAMA BEAR SAYS

Ask for help when you need it.
You are not a burden.
You are not interrupting.

Mama Bear Says

Light some candles
and dance by moonlight.

Mama Bear Says

Turn your face toward the sun.

Mama Bear Says

Light a candle when you
see the first star appear in
the night sky and call in
the Moon Bear.

MAMA BEAR SAYS

You are made
of Earth and Sea,
Sun and Moon.
You are the Divine
manifested in flesh.

Mama Bear Says

Take a long morning walk.

Mama Bear Says

Fill your dreams with
whimsy and delight.

Mama Bear Says

Cuddle with your beloved or a fur-baby.
Or be your own beloved.

MAMA BEAR SAYS

Embrace your imperfections.

Mama Bear Says

Create an altar for communing with your
ancestors. You are never alone.

MAMA BEAR SAYS

Wonder at the beauty
of your natural features.

Mama Bear Says

Share your day with
someone special.
Remember YOU are
someone special.

Mama Bear Says

Make every step a prayer
and every breath a celebration.

Mama Bear Says

Take one small step
toward your dream.

MAMA BEAR SAYS

No more hiding
your brilliance.

Mama Bear Says

Look at yourself in the mirror
and say, "I love you."

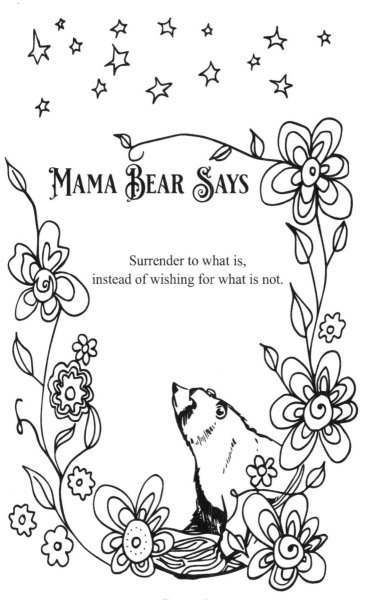

MAMA BEAR SAYS

Surrender to what is,
instead of wishing for what is not.

MAMA BEAR SAYS

The more you fill your thoughts
with positivity, the more
at peace you'll feel.

Mama Bear Says

Your inner light is shining bright.

Mama Bear Says

Choose to laugh and make
your heart drunk on life.

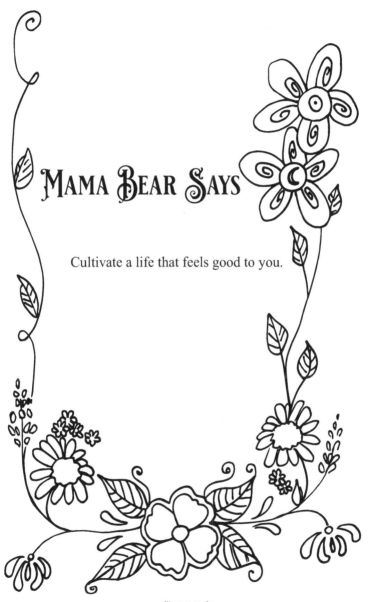

Mama Bear Says

Cultivate a life that feels good to you.

MAMA BEAR SAYS

Be yourself today.
You're beautiful like that.

MAMA BEAR SAYS

You are perfectly imperfect
and beautifully flawed.

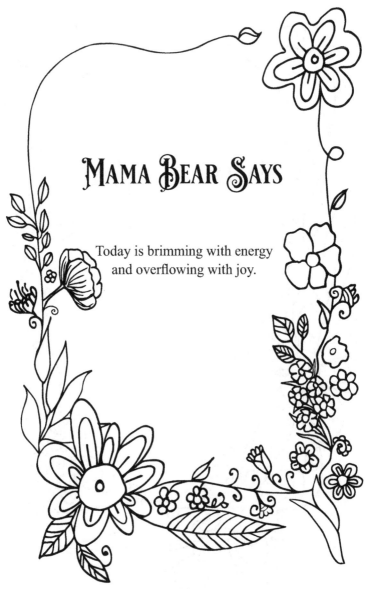

MAMA BEAR SAYS

Today is brimming with energy
and overflowing with joy.

MAMA BEAR SAYS

Forgive those who have harmed
you. It doesn't make it right,
and you don't have to forget.

Mama Bear Says

You get to choose
the contents of your life.

Mama Bear Says

You have the gift of choice.

MAMA BEAR SAYS

What you envision today
becomes your tomorrow.

Mama Bear Says

Obstacles are moving out of
your way and your path is
being made clear.

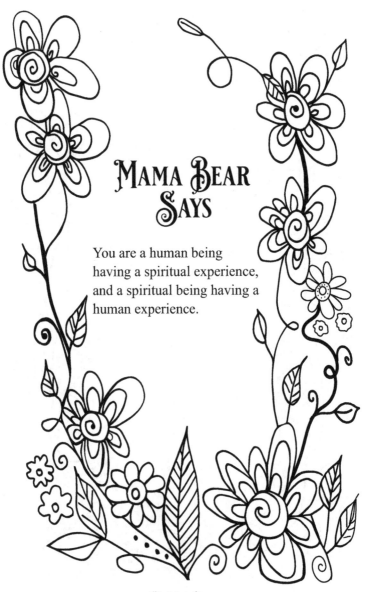

Mama Bear Says

You are a human being having a spiritual experience, and a spiritual being having a human experience.

Mama Bear Says

Your efforts are being
supported by the Universe.

Mama Bear Says

Your dreams are about to
manifest before your eyes.

MAMA BEAR SAYS

Nurture healthy relationships.

Mama Bear Says

Every morning this week,
wake up with thoughts and
feelings that nourish your soul.

MAMA BEAR SAYS

Beauty is everywhere in everything.

MAMA BEAR SAYS

Only compare yourself to
who you were yesterday.

MAMA BEAR SAYS

Look at the big picture.
Then, look at the details.

Mama Bear Says

Break it down
into smaller chunks.

MAMA BEAR SAYS

You've got this!

MAMA BEAR SAYS

Tell Your Story.
Write the words
on your heart.

MAMA BEAR SAYS

Listen to the silence
instead of filling it with noise.

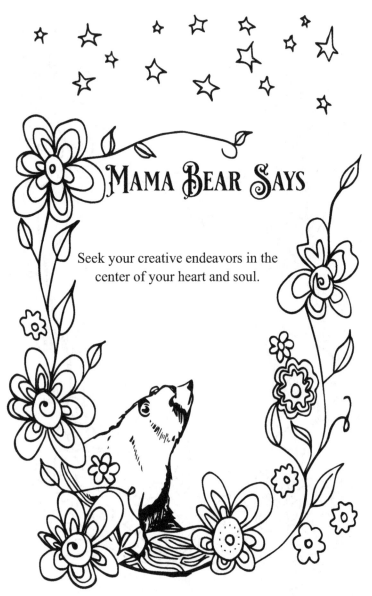

Mama Bear Says

Seek your creative endeavors in the
center of your heart and soul.

MAMA BEAR SAYS

Sit on the floor in your discomfort.
Here in the stillness, you'll hear the
comfort of your inner voice.

Mama Bear Says

Trust.

MAMA BEAR SAYS

Believe.

ᴀCKNOWLEDGMENTS

It takes a village to write and self-publish a book. To honor that village, I have to go back to elementary school. This book would not have materialized if not for the many teachers, mentors, and guides who encouraged me along the way. To these blessed Beings, I wholeheartedly thank you. Each of you represents a unique aspect of these writings.

To my incredibly supportive family, you have each left an indelible mark on my heart. To my sons who decided to take a journey with a wild and crazy witch, a deep bow of gratitude to both of you. I'm a better person because of you.

To the Wise Women with whom I circle, you helped me grow into the Mama Bear: Wendy, Cat, Francine, Jill, Jodi, Eddy, Pixie, Tracey, Cinnamon, Jules, Tiffanie, Connye, Jen, Kelly, Erin, and Sharon. To each of you, I send a Mama Bear hug and love.

To my Familiar, Marble, who often embodied Mama Bear, I miss you pretty girl.

Thank you to Mama Bear for showing up at exactly the right time to save my life. You've inhabited my dreams and showed me how to truly love who I am.

There are not enough words to honor and thank the Universe for its golden threads guiding me through the shadows when I had no light of my own to shine.

ABOUT HEATHER DAKOTA

Heather Dakota is a former Editor and Creative Manager with 25+ years experience in publishing. She has authored more than 75 books and is now coaching and designing for writers, healers, artists, herbalists, and magic makers to help them self-publish the book of their dreams. She is known as The Book Witch and Mama Bear. This book holds the wisdom that she works with to nurture her customers and clients, and now she shares it with you.

Heather is available for podcasts, interviews, and book events, please contact info@heatherdakota.com

MORE BY HEATHER

If you would like to amplify Mama Bear's wisdom, please leave a review at your favorite Online retailer, your social media platforms, and Goodreads. Thank you! **#mamabearsays**

For Writers:

Articles & freebies - www.heatherdakota.com/blog

Courses for writers and indie publishers at www.wisewomancollective.com

Writer's Quest - www.heatherdakota.com/writers-quest

Book Witch Planners, Notebooks & Journals coming September 2021

For Readers:

Look for the next Mama Bear book in March 2022.

For Indie Publishers:

www.heatherdakota.com/book-witching

For more Mama Bear Says™ wisdom,
magic, and book release dates,
sign up for the free mOOn newsletters at
www.heatherdakota.com